D0529454

SALAD DRESSINGS FOR LIFE . . .

from God's Garden

A Collection of 117 Recipes

by Rhonda J. Malkmus and friends

1

Salad Dressings for Life . . . from God's Garden

The nutritional and health information in this book is based on the teachings of God's Holy Word, the Bible, as well as research and personal experiences by the author and many others. The purpose of this book is to provide information and education about health. The author and publisher do not offer medical advice or prescribe the use of diet as a form or treatment for sickness without the approval of a health professional.

Because there is always some risk involved when changing diet and lifestyles, the author and publisher are not responsible for any adverse effects or consequences that might result. Please do not apply the techniques of this book if you are not willing to assume the risk.

If you do use the information contained in this book without the approval of a health professional, you are prescribing for yourself, which is your constitutional right, but the author and publisher assume no responsibility.

© Copyright 2002 by Rhonda J. Malkmus
All rights reserved

Library of Congress in Publication Data
Malkmus, Rhonda J.
>   *Salad Dressings for Life . . . from God's Garden -*
>   *A Collection of 117 Recipes*
>   1. Christian, 2. Recipes, 3. Health, 4. Raw Food

Library of Congress Catalog Card No. 2001131355
ISBN 0-929619-11-0

First Printing: 2002

Printed in the United States of America
All Bible quotations are taken from the authorized **King James Version**

Published and Distributed by

HALLELUJAH ACRES PUBLISHING
P.O. BOX 2388
SHELBY, NC 28151
(704) 481-1700

Visit our web site at http://www.hacres.com

Samples of responses that poured into Hallelujah Acres when we asked the question, "How about a salad dressing recipe book?"

"YES!!!! PLEASE DO A SALAD DRESSING RECIPE BOOK! We need a salad dressing recipe book! We are Health Ministers and one of the biggest and repeated questions are: But what can I put on my salads and veggies? We give them MANY ideas & even recipes but some still don't seem to get it. So if we had a salad dressing recipe book - they could make new dressings to their heart's content. And have no excuse that they just don't know what to put on their salads. There have been so many good salad dressing recipes that you have shared in the health tips this summer from your readers. Go for it, George & Rhonda - this is a winner!"

- Alan and Sandy Skoog, Casper, WY

"I'm always in search of great healthy salad dressings. If you publish a book, I'll be one of the first to buy it. Go for it. Thanks."

- Dale A. Schwartz

"I would also like to see a salad dressing cookbook! I am new at this, and so far I have only tried your Raspberry Vinaigrette recipe. It is a smashing success with all who have tried it so far!

"I am not 100% Hallelujah Diet yet, but am definitely working in that direction. I have never been a fruit / vegetable / salad person before, but since I have been doing this, I am surprised at how much I am enjoying raw fruits and especially vegetables."

- Rick Rice

"I've been hoping for months that you would publish all the wonderful salad dressing recipes in book form. I'll be looking for it soon!"

- Kathleen McKinney

"I think a collection of salad dressing recipes is an excellent idea, since salads are the foundation of our daily diet. And we do need variety. Having those dressings in one handy collection booklet would help us prepare a salad more quickly, especially if we're teetering on what exactly to prepare when we haven't given it prior thought. Also, we could easily mark the ones we prefer.

"I hardly ever eat store bought dressings. ninety-nine percent of the time we use a mixture of 3/4 Bragg's apple cider vinegar and 1/4 (or less to taste) Celtic Sea Salt to taste. It's tasty, but after 7 years some good tasting healthy recipes would make for a wonderful change! Here's hoping!"

- Ron Leonard

DEDICATION

This book is dedicated to all of the wonderful people who have made a difference in my life!

It is dedicated to my precious husband, George Malkmus, who is ever at my side encouraging me to press toward the mark.

To my family, living hundreds of miles away, but always an encouragement to me. They inspire me with their never-ending love and understanding!

To my awesome friends, who motivate me with their support, their prayers, and their love.

To the staff at Hallelujah Acres, who tirelessly give of themselves to help others on an ongoing basis.

To our wonderful Health Ministers around the world, who never tire of helping us reach the world with the message, *"You Don't Have to be Sick!"*

To everyone who follows The Hallelujah Diet and Lifestyle, who are regaining their health and saving their very lives by the choices they make.

Last, but certainly not least, this book is also dedicated to our Lord and Savior, Jesus Christ, that He might be lifted up, and that you may know Him as your personal Savior.

"Grace be unto you, and peace, from God our Father, and from the Lord Jesus Christ. I thank my God upon every remembrance of you, ..." Philippians 1:2-3

ACKNOWLEDGEMENTS

I give thanks with a grateful heart to:

My Lord and Savior, Jesus Christ, who through the power of the Holy Spirit gave me the vision to create these dressings and the strength and vision to complete this work.

My beloved husband, George, who always encourages me to give my best for God's service! His patience and understanding are my strength!

Ed Haymond, who used his precious time to proofread and edit and give advice about this manuscript. Also, Sarah Westbrook and Diane Vaillancourt, who also took time from their busy schedules to proofread and make many helpful suggestions.

Dennis Poteat, who took my manuscript and used his God-given talents of design and graphics to turn it into something to behold!

My friends from around the world, who have submitted recipes to be used in this book; their contributions help to create the endless ideas found in this book.

"I thank my God always on your behalf, for the grace of God which is given you by Jesus Christ; that in every thing ye are enriched by Him, in all utterance, and in all knowledge; Even as the testimony of Christ was confirmed in you."   *1 Corinthians 1:4-6*

BY THE GRACE OF GOD!

In 1981, an event happened in the twinkling of an eye that changed my life forever! It changed how I think, what is important to me, and who I am. On a rainy, foggy night I was driving along a rural road in Iowa. As my car approached an unmarked railroad crossing, my passenger yelled, "There's a train!" I slammed on the brakes and my car screeched to a halt and stalled inches from the railroad crossing. Realizing we were too close to the track, I took my foot off the brake to try to restart the engine and when I did, the car inched ever closer to the path of the oncoming train. Frantically, I tried to restart my car but to no avail. There we were with no time to escape, and I truly expected to meet the Lord that night.

After the initial impact, the car flew through the air. When the car landed and finally stopped rolling, the very first thought I had was, *"In everything give thanks, for this is the will of God in Christ Jesus concerning you" (I Thessalonians 5:18).* With fear and trembling, I thanked the Lord as my hand landed on the window crank. The train engineer had already run to my car, and I called to him to open the door, but he was in shock and thought we were dead, so he simply stood there staring. Imagine his shock when I rolled down the window and climbed out of the car and then opened the door and helped my passenger to safety. By the grace of God, my friend and I walked away from a potentially deadly accident!

We were rushed to the hospital, where we received many x-rays. The doctors were amazed that they could find no broken bones, only one small laceration and many bruises. However, in the days, weeks, and months that followed, I learned what an impact with a freight train can do to the human body. My fillings were shattered, as well as the enamel on many of my teeth. As a result of the accident, I developed arthritis in every joint of my body.

Almost overnight, pain had become my constant companion. The pain was so intense that there were days I thought going to heaven would have been easier than living. If I sat in a chair, I could hardly get up; if I stood any length of time, I could hardly sit down. I had to run hot water on my hands each morning before doing anything else to get them to function. My right elbow, which had been dislocated, ached constantly, and there wasn't an area in my spine that wasn't affected. Due to the pain often being almost unbearable, I was relatively inactive and this brought many unwanted pounds. Yet I knew God allowed this accident to happen for a reason, I just didn't know "the rest of the story."

By the fall of 1990, the arthritis was so severe that my doctor advised that I move to a milder climate. When I arrived in Tennessee, the first person I met was George Malkmus! Meeting George was the second collision in my life! But this one would bring joy and unveiling of God's purpose for my pain. George began to share with me that a changed diet and lifestyle would no doubt improve my life and health. With nothing to lose and everything to gain, I began to change my diet to The Hallelujah Diet, and over a period of time it truly did change my life. Today my health has been completely restored and I can now do things I could only dream about before. I am free of pain, walk over a mile daily on hilly terrain, and have lost over 80 pounds.

After experiencing the health a simple diet change can bring, hallelujah is a most appropriate word. Over the past several years, over a million others have changed their diet and lifestyle to The Hallelujah Diet, with many experiencing wonderful results. Our mission is to teach the world God's plan for our diet and health and to share with others, "You Don't Have to be Sick!"

(For more information on The Hallelujah Diet, see our web site and address on the back page.)

"The thief cometh not, but for to steal, and to kill, and to destroy: I am come that they might have life, and have it more abundantly." John 10:10

SALAD DRESSINGS FOR LIFE ... from God's Garden
TABLE OF CONTENTS

"What? Know ye not that your body is the temple of the Holy Ghost which is in you, which ye have of God, and ye are not your own? For ye are bought with a price: therefore glorify God in your body, and in your spirit, which are God's." I Corinthians 6:19-20

FOREWORD

For the past several years, I have been publishing a free electronic Health Tip, which currently is going into some 50,000 homes each week. One of the features of this Health Tip is a weekly recipe.

About a year ago, I asked our readers to send me their favorite salad dressing recipes, and I told them that if the recipe was exceptional, I would feature it in our weekly Health Tip. Well, the response was overwhelming, and we featured a different salad dressing recipe every week for many, many months.

Then one day I received a letter from one of our subscribers, suggesting that these salad dressing recipes be put into booklet form. I ran the thought past Rhonda, and she started to get excited about the prospect of such a book. So the next step was to find out if our Health Tip readers thought it was a good idea. Rhonda and I could hardly believe the letters we received; we were swamped with positive responses.

Rhonda immediately started compiling the recipes, breaking them down into their respective categories, and entering them into her computer. In addition to these salad dressing recipes, she added many that she has accumulated since writing her *Recipes for Life . . . from God's Garden* book in 1998.

Well, the project has been completed, and I want to thank all of the subscribers who sent in their favorite salad dressing recipes, and Rhonda for the many, many hours she put into making this book a reality. Since salads are such a big part of The Hallelujah Diet, I trust you will find the contents of this new book a help and blessing as you seek to tantalize the taste buds of both yourself and your family.

Yours for a Healthy World,

Rev. George H. Malkmus

"I beseech you therefore, brethren, by the mercies of God, that ye present your bodies a living sacrifice, holy, acceptable unto God, which is your reasonable service. And be not conformed to this world: but be ye transformed by the renewing of your mind, that ye may prove what is that good, and acceptable, and perfect will of God." Romans 12:1-2

INTRODUCTION

Welcome to the wonderful land of salad dressings!

It is my hope and prayer that your experience with this book will assist you in your journey into healthful eating, and that these recipes will bring you great joy as you seek to restore or maintain your God-given temple. I pray that the Lord will bless your efforts, and may each step you take bring you ever closer to Him!

At Hallelujah Acres, we teach that salads are the mainstay of The Hallelujah Diet. Therefore, I pray this new book will be a valuable tool in helping you to prepare delightful salads for your family. My book, *Recipes for Life . . . from God's Garden,* written in 1998, contains 25 salad dressing recipes, but many people have written expressing a desire for more salad dressings from which to choose.

May the recipes in this book serve as a guideline to help you attain your own creativity in the kitchen. Use them as a stepping stone to develop your own taste treats. Be adventuresome - try seasonings that are new to you, and sample new vegetables in their raw state just as they come from God's Garden. Don't get discouraged as you begin this new adventure into health. Remember that with God's help you can do anything!

Because He Lives,

Rhonda J. Malkmus

"I can do all things through Christ which strengtheneth me." Philippians 4:13

Before we begin our adventure into the wonderful land of salad dressings, I would like to share with you some suggestions for building a beautiful, palate-pleasing salad! Don't get bogged down preparing the *same* salad every day; use your imagination and create some truly beautiful salads. For additional ideas, see *Recipes for Life . . . from God's Garden* where I share 40 different ways to build a salad, plus several grain and vegetable salads for variety!

HOW TO BUILD A SALAD

1. Select green leafy lettuce, kale, spinach, endive, bok choy, or other dark leafy greens (never iceberg lettuce, which is devoid of many nutrients).
2. Wash, drain, and wrap greens in a clean towel (not a paper towel, since some are coated with formaldehyde), then place in refrigerator to crisp.
3. While greens are crisping, clean and prepare the rest of the vegetables, then set aside.
4. Remove chilled lettuce and other greens from towel and tear into bite-size pieces (using a knife bruises the lettuce).
5. Fill the serving bowls half full of greens, and then add layers of your favorite prepared vegetables.
6. Some vegetables to be considered:

· Small broccoli florets	· Radishes
· Finely chopped red onion	· Fresh asparagus
· Green onion or scallions	· Cherry or chopped tomatoes
· Small cauliflower florets	· Raw sweet corn
· Diced red or yellow bell peppers	· Raw snow peas
· Finely diced celery	· Grated sweet potatoes or yams
· Diced avocado	· Grated turnips
· Grated California carrots	· Grated jicama
· Grated zucchini	· Grated beets
· Grated yellow squash	· Red or green cabbage
· Sliced or diced cucumber	· Chopped regular or garlic chives
· Grated kohlrabi	· Minced parsley

Nuts and seeds that may be used when not using avocado are: sunflower seeds, chopped almonds, or pecans. (Using nuts, seeds, and avocados at the same time gives the body too much fat to digest at one meal.)

CAUTION :
THE CHOICE IS YOURS

As the reader will soon realize, several of the dressings that are contained in this book have been submitted by some of our *Back to the Garden* Newsletter, and *Hallelujah Health Tip* readers.

Some recipes may contain some ingredients that are not ideal. Readers will need to judge for themselves whether the ingredients in each recipe are something they would like to use. Substitutions can be made, or ingredients can be omitted, reduced or increased to suit the taste buds and preferences of each individual or family.

I encourage the reader to experiment, make substitutions, and find out what is most pleasing to your palate. This is an adventure that can change your life forever. Each new step you take can assist you in attaining and sustaining "Ultimate Health." May our Lord and Savior, Jesus Christ, bless and guide you and those you love as you seek to change your diet and lifestyle so that each of you can sustain or renew your strength like the eagle!

"Who satisfieth thy mouth with good things; so that thy youth is renewed like the eagle's." Psalm 103:5

SUBSTITUTIONS

· Replace distilled white vinegar, red wine, or balsamic vinegar with fresh lemon juice or raw organic, unpasteurized apple cider vinegar.

· Replace black pepper with organic herb blends or a little cayenne.

· Replace table salt with Celtic Sea Salt™ with no chemicals added nor nutrients removed, or Nama Shoyu™ organic, unpasteurized soy sauce.

· Replace cornstarch with arrowroot powder.

· Replace peanut butter with raw almond butter.

· Replace sugar with date sugar, dates, raw unfiltered honey, maple syrup granules, or stevia.

· Replace ground nuts with ground flaxseed on salads.

· Replace gelatin made from animal products with agar-agar, a natural gelling and thickening agent. To use, combine 1 tablespoon granulated or 2 tablespoons flaked agar-agar with $3^1/_2$ cups liquid prior to heating.

· Replace hydrogenated oils with cold-pressed extra virgin olive oil, raw flaxseed oil, or Udo's Choice Perfected Oil Blend™.

· Replace regular coconut with unsweetened, organic, shredded coconut.

· Replace regular raisins (which are usually sprayed with chemicals and then dried in the sun without sprayed-on pesticides removed) with organic raisins.

· Replace milk with almond or sunflower milk. (See *Recipes for Life. . . from God's Garden*)

13

AVOCADO BASED DRESSINGS

"And God said, Behold, I have given you every herb bearing seed, which is upon the face of all the earth, and every tree, in the which is the fruit of a tree yielding seed; to you it shall be for meat." Genesis 1:29

Avocado Tomato Dressing

2	ripe avocados, peeled and pitted
1	medium ripe tomato
1	teaspoon herb seasoning
$1/_4$	cup fresh lemon juice
$1/_2$	cup finely chopped red onion
	Celtic Sea Salt to taste (optional)

Place all ingredients except chopped red onion in blender and blend until smooth; fold in chopped onion.

Creamy Green Dressing
Karen Lemonds

$1/_2$	medium ripe avocado, peeled and pitted
$3/_4$	cup distilled water
3	tablespoons fresh lemon juice
$1/_4$	cup almonds, soaked overnight and drained
$1/_4$	teaspoon garlic powder
$1^1/_4$	teaspoons onion powder or flakes
	Celtic Sea Salt to taste (optional)

Blend all ingredients until smooth.

Avocado Mayo

1	cup pecans, minced
1	large, ripe Haas avocado or other avocado, peeled and pitted
1	tablespoon fresh lemon juice
2	tablespoons raw unfiltered apple cider vinegar
6	medium pitted dates or enough to equal 3 tablespoons, packed
1	teaspoon minced garlic
	Celtic Sea Salt to taste (optional)

Place all ingredients in blender and blend until a creamy consistency is reached.

Avocado Lemon Dressing

1	cup distilled water
$\frac{1}{2}$	cup almonds, soaked overnight and drained
$\frac{1}{4}$	cup fresh lemon juice
$\frac{1}{2}$	red, orange or yellow sweet medium bell pepper
1	teaspoon ground celery seed
1	ripe avocado, peeled and pitted
$\frac{1}{4}$	cup lemon zest (grated lemon rind)
$\frac{1}{2}$	cup fresh or $\frac{1}{4}$ cup dried sweet basil
1	tablespoon fresh or 1 teaspoon dried oregano
1	garlic clove, peeled
	Celtic Sea Salt to taste (optional)

Blend water and soaked almonds until smooth. Add remaining ingredients and blend well.

Guacamole Dressing

2   ripe avocados, peeled and pitted
1   ripe tomato
$1/_2$ cup red onion, diced
1   large garlic clove, peeled
$1/_3$ cup fresh cilantro leaves, tightly packed
2   tablespoons fresh lemon juice
       Celtic Sea Salt to taste (optional)

Place all ingredients in blender and blend until desired consistency.

Merry's Favorite Dressing
Merry M.

1   ripe avocado, peeled and pitted
1   garlic clove, peeled
1   lemon, juiced
       Celtic Sea Salt to taste (optional)
       Distilled water

Place avocado, garlic, lemon juice and seasoning in blender with enough water to cover halfway. Blend until creamy. Add water, if needed, to reach desired consistency.

Avocado Carrot Dressing

3   cups freshly extracted carrot juice
2   ripe avocados, peeled and pitted
1   garlic clove, peeled
1   teaspoon fresh parsley or $^1/_2$ teaspoon dried parsley
2   teaspoons dried oregano
3   scallions, minced
       Celtic Sea Salt to taste (optional)

Blend first five ingredients until smooth. Add Celtic Sea Salt to taste, chill and garnish with minced scallions when served.

Pesto Dressing

4   small garlic cloves, peeled
$2^2/_3$ cup tightly packed fresh basil leaves
$^1/_3$ cup pine nuts (pignolia)
$^1/_3$ cup cold-pressed extra virgin olive oil
           Celtic Sea Salt to taste (optional)

Place all ingredients except oil in food processor and process until chopped fine. With the machine running, slowly add oil through the feed tube. Stop machine and scrape sides of bowl, replace cover and continue to process until smooth.

Darlene's Favorite Dressing
Darlene Schnabel

$^1/_2$	ripe avocado, peeled and pitted
1	celery stalk
1	medium ripe tomato
$^1/_4$	cup fresh, snipped chives
$^1/_4$	cup fresh, snipped parsley
1	cup distilled water
$^1/_4$	cup raw unfiltered apple cider vinegar
2	teaspoons vegetable seasoning or herbs of choice

Combine all ingredients in a blender and blend until smooth. Chill before serving. Serves 4 – 6.

OIL BASED DRESSINGS

"For the Lord thy God bringeth thee into a good land, a land of brooks of water, of fountains and depths that spring out of the valleys and hills; A land of wheat, and barley, and vines, and fig trees, and pomegranates; a land of oil olive, and honey." Deuteronomy 8: 7-8

Garlic Dressing

1	cup cold-pressed extra virgin olive oil
3-4	medium garlic cloves, peeled
$1/_4$	teaspoon Celtic Sea Salt (optional)
$1/_4$	teaspoon dill weed
$1/_2$	cup fresh lemon juice

Place all ingredients in a blender and process on high speed until creamy.

Our Favorite Dressing
Rosemary Anderson

$2/_3$	cup raw unfiltered apple cider vinegar
$2/_3$	cup cold-pressed extra virgin olive oil
$1/_4$	cup distilled water
2	teaspoons Dijon mustard (optional)
2	tablespoons raw unfiltered honey
$1/_4$	teaspoon cayenne pepper (optional)
$1/_2$	teaspoon dried basil
$1/_2$	teaspoon dried oregano
1	clove garlic, peeled and minced

Combine in bowl and whisk for several minutes until blended.

Poppy Seed Dressing
Julie Wandling

$2/_3$ cup raw unfiltered honey
$1/_2$ teaspoon dry mustard (optional)
$1/_2$ teaspoon kelp or 1/8 teaspoon Celtic Sea Salt
$1/_8$ cup raw unfiltered apple cider vinegar
$1/_2$ red onion, quartered
$1/_2$ cup cold-pressed extra virgin olive oil
$1/_2$ tablespoon poppy seeds

Put all ingredients in the blender and whiz until the onion has disappeared.

Ellinor's Dressing
Ellinor L. Nightingale

1   cup raw unfiltered apple cider vinegar
$1/_3$ cup balsamic vinegar
$1/_3$ cup cold-pressed extra virgin olive oil
1   tablespoon raw unfiltered honey
1   teaspoon mixed herb seasoning or your own seasoning.

Combine in a glass jar with tight fitting lid. Shake together and apply to salad.

Sue's Smoky Tomato Dressing
Sue Stahly

3	tablespoons cold-pressed extra virgin olive oil
1	teaspoon Celtic Sea Salt
1	tablespoon tahini
1	tablespoon lemon juice
$^1/_2$	teaspoon saltless barbecue flavoring (optional)
1	teaspoon Salt-Free Spike™
1-2	tomatoes, peeled
Dash	Liquid Smoke™

Adding sun-dried tomatoes is a delicious way as well!

Place all ingredients in food processor or blender and blend! The result is a thick creamy smoky delicious tomato dressing!

Sherfinski Favorite Dressing
Marge and Val Sherfinski

On each salad serving drizzle:

1	tablespoon Udo's Choice Perfected Oil Blend™ (or to taste)
1	tablespoon balsamic vinegar (or to taste)

Drizzle on the big veggies first; mix and enjoy.

Herb Vinaigrette Dressing

$1/_3$ cup fresh lemon juice
$1/_2$ teaspoon dried basil (if using fresh, use twice as much)
1   teaspoon dried oregano or tarragon (if using fresh, use twice as much)
$1/_4$ teaspoon Celtic Sea Salt
$1/_2$ teaspoon dry mustard (optional)
$1/_2$ cup fresh Italian parsley, minced
$1/_2$ cup cold-pressed sunflower oil or Udo's Choice Perfected Oil Blend™
$1/_2$ cup cold-pressed extra virgin olive oil
1   garlic clove, peeled

Combine, in a jar, all ingredients except oils and shake well. Add oils and shake again, discard garlic.

Note: May also want to add one or more of the following:
1   tablespoon fresh rosemary, minced
1   tablespoon fresh cilantro leaves, minced
3   tablespoons fresh thyme

Italian Caesar Dressing
Zolla Michalak

2   tablespoons cold-pressed extra virgin olive oil
$1/_4$ teaspoon dried parsley
$1/_4$ teaspoon dried oregano
$1/_4$ teaspoon dried basil
$1/_4$ teaspoon garlic powder
$1/_2$ capful raw unfiltered apple cider vinegar
$1/_4$ teaspoon Vegenaise™ (or to taste)
     Celtic Sea Salt to taste (optional)

Place all ingredients, mix well, chill and serve.

Italian Dressing

$1/_2$ cup cold-pressed extra virgin olive oil
$1/_4$ cup fresh lemon juice
1-2   garlic clove, peeled
1   teaspoon whole grain mustard seed (optional)
$1/_2$ cup distilled water
1   green onion, chopped
1   teaspoon raw unfiltered honey or pure maple syrup
Dash   cayenne (or to taste)

Place all ingredients in a blender and blend until smooth. Remove from blender and add 2 teaspoons Italian seasoning or 1 teaspoon oregano and $1/_2$ teaspoon basil. Mix well. Refrigerate until used.

Zesty Italian Dressing
Valerie R. Samms

1   cup cold-pressed extra virgin olive oil
$1/_2$ cup Udo's Choice Perfected Oil Blend™ or other mild oil
$1/_2$ cup raw unfiltered apple cider vinegar or lemon juice
7-10   garlic cloves, peeled and pressed
1   green onion, chopped fine
$1/_4$ teaspoon ground celery seed
$1/_4$ teaspoon paprika
1   tablespoon raw unfiltered honey
$1/_2$ teaspoon molasses
$1/_2$ teaspoon dried basil
$1/_4$ teaspoon dried thyme
$1/_2$ teaspoon dried oregano
$1/_4$ teaspoon cayenne (optional)
    Celtic Sea Salt to taste (optional)

Combine ingredients in a jar and shake well. Refrigerate overnight before serving.

Greek Salad Dressing

Fill salad dressing bottle $^1/_3$ with cold-pressed extra virgin olive oil
Fill it to $^2/_3$ with tarragon vinegar (see Glossary of Ingredients)
Add the following:

1	garlic clove peeled, smashed or chopped
1	teaspoon herb seasoning
$^1/_2$	teaspoon brown spicy mustard (optional)
1	tablespoon raw unfiltered honey
	Celtic Sea Salt to taste (optional)

Cover and shake well.

Linda's Salad Dressing
Linda Leech

$^1/_4$	cup raw unfiltered apple cider vinegar
$^1/_2$	cup cold-pressed extra virgin olive oil or flaxseed oil*
1	large garlic clove, peeled and cut into quarters
1	tablespoon dried basil flakes
1	teaspoon onion powder
1	teaspoon all-purpose seasoning
$^1/_2$	teaspoon kelp (if desired)

Place all ingredients in a salad cruet container and shake to mix. Marinate several hours to several days. No one can resist its wonderful aroma!

*If using olive oil, don't refrigerate. If using flaxseed oil - refrigerate in a container that won't allow light to enter.

Tip: To counteract the effects of garlic, leafy green vegetables will sweeten your breath.

Tamari Dressing
Submitted anonymously by one of our readers

I make this dressing daily so it makes enough for one large salad bowl.

3	tablespoons cold-pressed extra virgin olive oil
1	tablespoon tamari
1	tablespoon tahini
Dash	red wine vinegar (or to taste)
Dash	fresh lemon juice (or to taste)
Dash	garlic powder

Stir well and toss in salad! Delicious!

Basil - Green Onion Dressing

1	cup fresh basil leaves
$1/_2$	cup cold-pressed extra virgin olive oil
$1/_4$	cup fresh lemon juice
4	green onions
2	ounces dehydrated tomatoes
2	garlic clove, peeled
$1/_8$	teaspoon cayenne (optional)
1	teaspoon raw unfiltered honey

Place all ingredients in blender or food processor and blend until creamy.

Carrot - Flaxseed Dressing

3   tablespoons flaxseed, soaked overnight in distilled water & drained*
1   cup fresh carrot juice or mixed vegetable juice
1   red, yellow or other sweet bell pepper, seeded and cut in chunks
$1/_4$ cup flaxseed oil
Dash cayenne (optional)
       Celtic Sea Salt to taste (optional)

*Save soaking water. In a blender, combine flaxseeds and their soak water, carrot juice, bell pepper and cayenne, then blend to desired consistency. Cover and refrigerate for at least an hour to allow flavors to blend. Thoroughly mix before using. Best used within 24 hours.

Note: May also want to add your favorite herb mixture or $1/_2$ cup celery leaves, minced or $1/_2$ ripe avocado, diced.

Sun-Dried Tomato Dressing
Laura Krewson

$1/_3$ cup fresh lemon juice
$1/_3$ cup raw unfiltered honey
$1/_3$ cup oil (half Udo's Choice Perfected Oil Blend™ and half cold-pressed extra virgin olive oil)
1-2   garlic cloves, peeled
$1/_2$ teaspoon dried basil
1   teaspoon dried oregano
8-10   sun-dried tomatoes, chopped
       Celtic Sea Salt to taste (optional)

Mix all ingredients. Keeps well in the refrigerator.

Sea Vegetable Dressing

1   cup cold-pressed extra virgin olive oil
$^1/_4$ teaspoon powdered kelp or other sea vegetable
$^1/_2$ lemon, juiced
         Raw unfiltered honey to taste

Place all ingredients into blender and process until smooth; add herbs to taste.

Tahini Dressing
D. A. and R. E. Carrigan

$^1/_4$ cup fresh lemon juice
$^1/_2$ cup Udo's Choice Perfected Oil Blend™, flaxseed, or cold-pressed extra virgin olive oil
$^1/_3$ cup tahini
1   tablespoon onion, finely chopped
1   garlic clove, peeled
1   tablespoon pure maple syrup
$^1/_4$ cup distilled water
         Celtic Sea Salt to taste (optional)

Combine all ingredients in a blender and blend till smooth.

Dill Dressing

$1/2$	cup cold-pressed extra virgin olive oil or Udo's Choice Perfected Oil Blend™
$1/4$	cup fresh lemon juice
1	tablespoon dill, snipped
1-2	tablespoons chives, snipped
$1/4$	teaspoon herbs of choice (optional)
1	garlic clove, peeled and halved
	Celtic Sea Salt to taste (optional)

Combine all ingredients except oil. Whisk oil in slowly until well combined. Cover and refrigerate overnight. Remove and discard garlic clove halves before serving.

Creamy Dill Dressing

1	cup distilled water
1	cup cold-pressed extra virgin olive oil, Udo's Choice Perfected Oil Blend™, other flaxseed oil or combination
$1^1/2$	teaspoons dill weed
2	teaspoons onion powder
$1^1/4$	cup rice milk or other milk substitute
1	small garlic clove, peeled
$1/2$	cup fresh lemon juice

Blend all ingredients except lemon juice. Stir in lemon juice and chill before serving.

Gerald's Dill Dressing
Gerald Pedersen

$1/2$ cup cold-pressed extra virgin olive oil
$1/4$ cup fresh lemon juice
$1/8$ teaspoon garlic powder
$1/2$ teaspoon salt-free seasoning
$1/4$ teaspoon cayenne pepper (optional) or herb seasoning
$1/4$ teaspoon raw unfiltered honey
$3/4$ teaspoon dill weed

Put everything in a jar. Shake vigorously. Chill. Shake again before serving.

George's Favorite Dressing

1   tablespoon Udo's Choice Perfected Oil Blend™
1   tablespoon cold-pressed extra virgin olive oil
1   tablespoon distilled water
1   teaspoon fresh lemon, orange juice, or raw unfiltered apple cider vinegar
$1/2$ teaspoon all purpose herb blend
1   teaspoon onion flakes

Place all ingredients in a bowl and mix well. Marinate ten to fifteen minutes for flavors to blend. Amount of each ingredient may be varied to satisfy individual tastebuds.

Chris' Favorite Dressing
Chris Phillips

1   cup cold-pressed extra virgin olive oil
3   tablespoons raw unfiltered apple cider vinegar
3   tablespoons raw unfiltered honey
1   teaspoon garlic powder (or garlic clove peeled and minced)
1   teaspoon Italian herb seasoning
        Celtic Sea Salt to taste (optional)

Pour all ingredients into a salad dressing jar and shake vigorously. Refrigerate. This dressing becomes better with age!

Mountain Dressing

1   cup cold-pressed extra virgin olive oil
4-5   garlic cloves, peeled and chopped
$^1/_2$ cup sesame seeds
        Celtic Sea Salt to taste (optional)

Mix thoroughly, cover and refrigerate for several hours to allow flavors to mingle.

Cabbage Slaw Dressing
Anthea Dedericks
South Africa

1   cup raw unfiltered apple cider vinegar
1   cup cold-pressed extra virgin olive oil
2   tablespoons raw unfiltered honey (more or less to taste)
2   teaspoons garlic clove, peeled and chopped (important for flavor)
    Celtic Sea Salt or vegetable seasoning to taste

Shake together in a bottle and serve. Will keep a long time in the refrigerator and improves with age.

Flaxseed Oil Dressing
Ruth Wiedenhoeft

1   cup flaxseed oil (or cold-pressed extra virgin olive oil)
1   tablespoon basil (or a mixture of Italian herbs)
1   teaspoon granulated garlic (or 1 garlic clove, peeled and minced)
1   tablespoon dried onion flakes
    Celtic Sea Salt to taste (optional)

Mix with a hand blender or shake in a jar.

Lemon Herb Dressing

$^1/_3$ cup fresh lemon juice
$^1/_3$ cup raw unfiltered honey
$^1/_3$ cup cold-pressed extra virgin olive oil
1   garlic clove, peeled and minced
$^1/_2$ teaspoon dried basil (or 1 teaspoon fresh, if available)
1   teaspoon dried oregano (or 2 teaspoons fresh, if available)
1   tablespoon minced red onion
    Celtic Sea Salt to taste (optional)

Mince garlic and onion and combine with other liquids. Marinate for several hours in the refrigerator before serving.

Matt's Favorite Dressing
Matt Elzea

1   cup cold-pressed extra virgin olive oil
$^3/_4$ cup raw unfiltered apple cider vinegar
2   tablespoons raw unfiltered honey
3   garlic cloves, peeled and minced
$^1/_2$ teaspoon dried basil
$^1/_2$ teaspoon dried cilantro
$^1/_2$ teaspoon dried oregano
$^1/_2$ teaspoon dried thyme
    Celtic Sea Salt to taste (optional)

Combine all ingredients, mix or shake until all ingredients are well blended. For best flavor, marinate in the refrigerator for several hours.

Orange - Tahini Dressing

$^3/_4$ cup cold-pressed extra virgin olive oil
$^1/_2$ cup fresh orange juice
2   tablespoons tahini
          Celtic Sea Salt to taste (optional)

Place ingredients in blender and blend until smooth.

Lemon Dressing

4   teaspoons almonds or pecans, soaked overnight, drained, dried,
          and finely ground
2   tablespoons lemon juice
4   tablespoons cold-pressed extra virgin olive oil

Mix ground nuts with lemon juice, then add olive oil. Pour into a blender and process or use whisk and beat into a cream. To vary the flavor of this dressing, fold in your favorite herb mixture after removing from the blender.

Zesty Garlic Dressing
Valerie R. Samms

Run the following ingredients through your GreenStar™ or Champion™ juicer:

$^1/_2$	cup celery
1	lemon plus peel
5	garlic cloves, peeled (more or less to taste)
1	piece ginger (thumb size)
1	red bell pepper, halved and seeded

Combine juices in a bowl and fold in:

$^1/_2$	cup cold-pressed extra virgin olive oil or flaxseed oil
1-2	lemons, juiced by hand
	herb seasoning to taste

Add any other seasoning of your choice (garlic powder, onion powder, Celtic Sea Salt, etc.)

Tomato Dressing

1	medium ripe tomato
$^1/_2$	cup cold-pressed extra virgin olive oil
$^1/_4$	cup fresh lemon juice
2	garlic cloves, peeled
$^1/_2$	red onion, chopped
2	tablespoons raw unfiltered honey
	Celtic Sea Salt to taste (optional)

Place all ingredients in a blender and blend until desired consistency is reached. After blending, may add favorite herbs to enhance flavors.

Tomato Dressing for Two
Madeleine Sutherland
Perth, Australia

2   medium ripe tomatoes
1   garlic clove, peeled and crushed
$^1/_2$ teaspoon kelp granules
$^1/_4$ - $^1/_2$ cup Udo's Choice Perfected Oil Blend™ or cold-pressed extra
        virgin olive oil
        Lemon juice or raw unfiltered apple cider vinegar (optional)

Place all ingredients in a blender and process until smooth. For thinner consistency, add distilled water or more oil. May also include avocado, celery or cucumber for taste variation. Serve separately or mix through salad.

Habel's Favorite Dressing
Sylvie Habel
Quebec, Canada

4   tablespoons raw unfiltered apple cider vinegar
1   garlic clove, peeled
$^1/_4$ teaspoon onion powder
4   slices sun-dried tomatoes (homemade, of course), reconstituted
$^1/_2$ cup Udo's Choice Perfected Oil Blend™ or cold-pressed extra
        virgin olive oil
        Celtic Sea Salt to taste (optional)

Place all the ingredients in a blender and blend at medium speed. Add the oil *SLOWLY* through the opening in the cover to emulsify. Enjoy!

Gerald's Italian Dressing
Gerald Pedersen

1	cup cold-pressed extra virgin olive oil
$1/_4$	cup fresh lemon juice
$1/_4$	cup raw unfiltered apple cider vinegar
1	teaspoon salt-free seasoning
$1/_2$	teaspoon raw unfiltered honey
$1/_2$	teaspoon dried oregano
$1/_2$	teaspoon dry mustard
$1/_2$	teaspoon onion powder
$1/_2$	teaspoon paprika
$1/_8$	teaspoon dried thyme
1	clove garlic, peeled and crushed

Put all ingredients in a jar or bottle. Shake well and chill.

Healthy Oil and Vinegar Dressing
Chuck Irsak

3	parts raw flaxseed oil
2	parts raw unfiltered apple cider vinegar
1-2	parts raw unfiltered honey (to taste)

I usually mix this right onto my salad when I'm ready to eat it. I have never tried to store it so I don't know how that would work.

Hint: If you measure out the oil on a tablespoon first, and then the honey, the honey will roll right off of the spoon, making clean-up really easy.

Italian Basil Dressing
Catherine Lennon

2	ripe tomatoes
2	cups fresh basil, firmly packed
$1/_2$	cup almonds, soaked 12-48 hours and blanched to remove skin
2	tablespoons cold-pressed extra virgin olive oil
1	garlic clove, minced
	Celtic Sea Salt to taste (optional)

In a blender, mix all ingredients adding enough distilled water to reach a smooth and creamy consistency. Adjust seasonings to taste.

Sweet and Sour Dressing
Rose Mary King

5	parts extra virgin olive oil or Udo's Choice Perfected Oil Blend™
5	parts raw unfiltered honey
3	parts raw unfiltered apple cider vinegar

Note: May also want to add a favorite spice, such as all-purpose seasoning. Mix well before serving.

Mint Dressing

1 1/2   cups cold-pressed extra virgin olive oil, walnut oil or other unrefined oil
1/2   cup raw unfiltered apple cider vinegar or fresh lemon juice
1   cup fresh mint leaves, packed tightly
1   garlic clove, peeled and quartered
2   teaspoons raw unfiltered honey
    Herbs to taste

Place all ingredients in a blender and mix well.

Whitney's Delight Dressing
Cindy Russell

2   tablespoons brewers yeast
2   tablespoons nutritional yeast
2   tablespoons Udo's Choice Perfected Oil Blend™
2   tablespoons raw unfiltered apple cider vinegar
    Celtic Sea Salt to taste (optional)
    Enough distilled water to make it the consistency of dressing

Mix well. Pour over salad. Add less water to make it a thicker consistency and use for vegetable dip.

Unusual taste, but addicting! (And there are your B vitamins for the day.)

Ginger-Lime Dressing

$1/_4$ cup fresh lime juice
$1/_4$ cup mild oil such as Udo's Choice Perfected Oil Blend™, grapeseed or sesame seed
$1/_4$ cup distilled water
1   tablespoon fresh mint
1   tablespoon fresh cilantro
1   teaspoon ginger root, minced
2   teaspoons raw unfiltered honey or pure maple syrup
Dash   cayenne (optional)
       Celtic Sea Salt to taste (optional)

Place all ingredients in a blender and mix well.

Honey-Poppy Seed Dressing

1   cup raw unfiltered honey
1   teaspoon dry mustard (optional)
1   teaspoon paprika
2   teaspoons poppy seeds
3   teaspoons raw unfiltered apple cider vinegar
3   teaspoons fresh lemon juice
1   teaspoon grated red onion (optional)
1   cup cold-pressed extra virgin olive oil
       Celtic Sea Salt to taste (optional)

Place all ingredients in a blender except oil and blend to mix. With blender running, gradually add the oil until the mixture thickens. Store in a covered jar.

Honey Mustard Dressing
Carolyn Hall

$\frac{1}{4}$ cup Udo's Choice Perfected Oil Blend™ or flaxseed oil
$\frac{1}{4}$ cup cold-pressed extra virgin olive oil
$\frac{1}{4}$ cup distilled water
1   teaspoon dry mustard
1   wedge red onion
2-3   tablespoons raw unfiltered honey
4-6   almonds, soaked overnight, drained and chopped fine
$\frac{1}{4}$ cup or slightly less raw unfiltered apple cider vinegar
    Celtic Sea Salt to taste (optional)

Place all ingredients in a blender and process until smooth. Refrigerate and enjoy!

Note: Add or decrease amount of each ingredient to suit taste.

Julia's Honey Mustard Dressing
Julia Biedinger

$\frac{1}{2}$ cup raw unfiltered honey
$\frac{1}{4}$-$\frac{1}{2}$ cup brown mustard
$\frac{1}{2}$ cup cold-pressed extra virgin olive oil
2-3   tablespoons distilled water

Mix the honey, mustard and olive oil until completely blended. Slowly add the distilled water to reach desired consistency.

French Dressing

$^1/_2$ cup cold-pressed extra virgin olive oil
$^1/_2$ cup Udo's Choice Perfected Oil Blend™ or flaxseed oil
$^1/_3$ cup fresh lemon juice
$^1/_3$ cup raw unfiltered honey
1   tablespoon paprika
$^3/_4$ cup salt free tomato puree
1   tablespoon onion powder
$^1/_2$ teaspoon garlic powder
     Celtic Sea Salt to taste (optional)

Blend all ingredients on high for about 30 seconds. Chill in covered container before serving.

French-Tomato Dressing

$^1/_2$ cup cold-pressed extra virgin olive oil
$^1/_4$ cup fresh lemon juice
2   tablespoons raw unfiltered honey
1   small ripe tomato, quartered or 6 cherry tomatoes
$^1/_4$ cup organic salt free tomato paste
3   tablespoons distilled water
$^1/_2$ teaspoon onion flakea
     Celtic Sea Salt to taste (optional)

Place all ingredients in a blender and blend well. Cover and chill before serving.

Russian Dressing
Sarah Gilbert

$1^1/_2$	cups organic tomato juice or tomato sauce, salt free
$^1/_2$	cup cold-pressed extra virgin olive oil
$1^1/_2$	teaspoons dried basil
$1^1/_2$	teaspoons dried oregano
$^1/_2$	teaspoon dried thyme
$^1/_2$	teaspoon mustard (optional)
2	tablespoons tahini

Place all ingredients in a blender and blend for half a minute. After removing from blender, may fold in finely chopped green onion. Chill before serving.

Chunky Tomato Dressing

$^1/_2$	cup distilled water
$^1/_2$	cup Udo's Choice Perfected Oil Blend™, cold-pressed extra virgin olive oil or flaxseed oil
2	garlic cloves, peeled
1	teaspoon ground celery seed
$^1/_4$	teaspoon cayenne pepper (optional)
1	tablespoon minced red onion
1	teaspoon dried oregano
2	tablespoons hulled (white) sesame seeds
$^1/_4$	cup ripe (red or yellow) bell pepper, chopped
$^1/_4$	cup celery leaves
1	large ripe tomato, peeled and chopped into small bite-size pieces Celtic Sea Salt to taste (optional)

Place all ingredients except tomato in blender and process until smooth. When blended pour into container and fold in chopped tomato.

Note: May include $^1/_4$ of the tomato in blended ingredients, if desired.

Chef Paul's Italian Dressing
Chef Bill Paul

1   cup balsamic vinegar
1   cup cold-pressed extra virgin olive oil
2   tablespoons Italian seasoning
1   tablespoon fresh garlic, peeled and chopped

Place all ingredients in a covered jar and shake well.

SEED AND NUT BASED DRESSINGS

"And Jesus said unto them, Because of your unbelief: for verily I say unto you, If ye have faith as a grain of mustard seed, ye shall say unto this mountain, Remove hence to yonder place; and it shall remove; and nothing shall be impossible unto you." Matthew 17:20

Author's note: Nuts and seeds are soaked overnight to begin the sprouting process, which helps make them more digestible. If in a hurry, these recipes may be made without soaking nuts and seeds. However, be aware that seeds and nuts that are not soaked require the digestive system to work harder.

Nut and Tomato Dressing

3-4   ripe tomatoes
4   ounces nuts (walnuts, almonds, or pecans), soaked overnight
        and drained
        freshly extracted orange juice

Blend tomatoes until liquid, add nuts and continue processing until nuts are ground. Add freshly squeezed orange juice until desired consistency and flavor is reached.

Nut Butter and Garlic Dressing

$3/4$ cup nut butter or tahini
$1^1/_2$ cups distilled water
4-5   fresh garlic cloves, peeled and minced
3   medium ripe tomatoes
1   tablespoon fresh dillweed, chopped
       Celtic Sea Salt to taste (optional)

Combine all ingredients in a blender and blend on high for several minutes.

Orange Poppy Seed Dressing

2   tablespoons fresh orange juice
2   tablespoons distilled water
2   tablespoons fresh lemon juice
$1/4$ cup dates, pitted and chopped
$1/2$ cup almonds, grind to fine meal, soak overnight, drain & dry
$1/2$ teaspoon paprika
$1/2$ teaspoon ground celery seed
1   cup unsweetened pineapple juice
1-2   tablespoons poppy seeds

Place all ingredients except poppy seeds in a blender and process until well blended. Remove from blender and stir in poppy seeds. Chill before serving.

Sesame Seed Dressing

1   cup sesame seeds, soaked overnight and drained
2   cups distilled water (for soaking seeds)

Soak seeds overnight in distilled water. After soaking seeds overnight, drain and discard water. Place soaked sesame seeds in a blender with all other ingredients and blend until creamy.

$^1/_2$ cup distilled water
$^1/_4$ cup fresh parsley
$^1/_4$ cup fresh green onion
1   tablespoon garlic, minced
1   tablespoon fresh dill leaves
1   tablespoon fresh basil leaves
$^1/_4$ cup cold-pressed extra virgin olive oil
$^1/_3$ cup fresh lemon juice
            Celtic Sea Salt to taste (optional)

Almond Cucumber Dressing

Blend two large cucumbers. Add soaked almonds until desired consistency is reached. Add herb seasoning if desired.

Sunflower Cream Dressing

1 $\frac{1}{2}$ cups sunflower seeds
2   cups distilled water
$\frac{1}{2}$ cup fresh lemon juice
$\frac{1}{2}$ teaspoon garlic powder
1   teaspoon dehydrated onion flakes
1   tablespoon chopped chives
     Celtic Sea Salt to taste (optional)

Place all ingredients except chives in a blender and blend until smooth.
Fold in chives, cover and chill.

Note: May also want to add in one or more of the following: avocado,
minced red onion, or diced tomatoes.

Good on baked potatoes.

Creamy Ranch Dressing
Jolene Trickle

1   cup distilled water
1   cup almonds, soaked overnight and drained
1   teaspoon dried basil
1   teaspoon onion flakes or powder
$\frac{1}{2}$ teaspoon garlic powder
1   teaspoon raw unfiltered honey
3   tablespoons fresh lemon juice
     Celtic sea salt to taste (optional)

Blend almonds and water in blender until smooth. Remove from blender
and fold in seasonings and lemon juice. Chill before serving.

Pecan Dressing

3   ounces pecans, soaked overnight and drained
2-3   medium ripe tomatoes, quartered
1-2   green onions or handful of fresh chives, chopped
$^1/_2$ cup fresh celery juice
1   teaspoon chervil or other herb of your choice

Combine all ingredients in a food processor or blender and process until smooth.

Basil-Garlic Dressing

$^1/_2$ cup almonds, soaked overnight and drained
$^1/_2$ cup distilled water
$^1/_4$ - $^1/_2$ cup chopped fresh basil leaves
1-2   garlic clove, peeled
$^1/_4$ lemon, peeled, seeded and chopped
1   teaspoon dried oregano
Dash   Celtic Sea Salt (optional)
Dash   cayenne (optional)

Combine almonds and distilled water in a blender and blend until smooth. Add remaining ingredients and blend to desired consistency. If not thick enough, add a few ground sunflower or flax seeds. If too thick, add more distilled water.

Festive Red Sauce
Gwen Lemonds

$3/_4$ cup hulled, raw sunflower seeds, soaked overnight and drained
$1^1/_2$ cups distilled water
$1/_2$ cup chopped red or green cabbage
2   garlic cloves, peeled
1   medium raw beet, peeled and sliced
1   lemon, juiced (about $1/_4$ cup)
    Celtic Sea Salt to taste (optional)

Place seeds in a blender and process until finely ground. Stop blender and scrape sides to loosen meal with knife blade or rubber spatula. Add distilled water, cabbage, garlic and beets. Whiz until smooth. Add Celtic Sea Salt and lemon juice and blend again until smooth.

Nut Mayonnaise

$1/_2$ cup walnuts, almonds or pecans, soaked overnight and drained
$1/_2$ cup distilled water
1-2   garlic cloves, peeled (to taste)
2   tablespoons fresh lemon juice
2   tablespoons pure maple syrup
Dash   Celtic Sea Salt (optional)
    Herb seasoning to taste
    Small amount of olive oil to taste

Place all ingredients in a blender and process until smooth. May be eaten as is, or try adding onion, parsley and more herb seasoning. Can be used as a dressing/sandwich spread for chopped/sliced raw veggies such as zucchini, bell pepper, shredded cabbage, carrot, etc. If dressing is not thick enough, add more nuts.

Excellent Nut Dressing

$^1/_2$ cup chopped walnuts, soaked overnight and drained
$^1/_2$ cup chopped almonds, soaked overnight and drained
6   cups carrots, grated
3   cups celery, chopped
$^1/_2$ teaspoon dried sage
        Cold-pressed extra virgin olive oil or Udo's Choice Perfected Oil Blend™

Place walnuts, almonds, grated carrots, celery and sage into blender; blend until smooth. Add oil until desired consistency is reached. Remove from blender and fold in the following; saving a small amount for garnish:

$^1/_4$ cup parsley, finely chopped
$^1/_2$ cup red onion, minced
$^3/_4$ cup pecans, coarsely chopped

Nut and Seed Dressing

1   cup distilled water
$^1/_2$ cup fresh lemon juice
$^1/_2$ cup almonds, soaked overnight and drained
1   cup sunflower seeds, soaked overnight and drained
1-2   teaspoons of raw unfiltered honey
1   garlic clove, peeled
1   teaspoon powdered rosemary
$^1/_4$ cup red onion
Pinch cayenne pepper (optional)
        Celtic Sea Salt to taste (optional)

Place all ingredients in a blender and process until smooth. Shut off machine, scrape sides and blend again if needed.

Pine Nut Dressing

$3/_4$ cup pignolia (pine nuts), chopped
$1/_4$ cup cold-pressed extra virgin olive oil
$1/_4$ teaspoon lemon zest (grated lemon rind)
2-3   tablespoons Tarragon vinegar (see Glossary of Ingredients)
Pinch   nutmeg

Combine all ingredients and mix thoroughly.

Cucumber Dressing

1   large cucumber, peeled and chopped in large chunks
2   green onions including tops
1   tablespoon fresh lemon juice
1   teaspoon onion flakes
$1/_2$ cup raw sunflower seeds, soaked overnight and drained
        Celtic Sea Salt to taste (optional)

Place all ingredients in blender and blend until smooth. For a thinner dressing, add a small amount of distilled water.

Coleslaw Dressing

$1/4$ cup distilled water
$1/2$ cup almonds, soaked overnight and drained
1   tablespoon caraway seeds
1   teaspoon raw unfiltered honey
$1/4$ cup fresh lemon juice
    Celtic Sea Salt to taste (optional)

Blend almonds and distilled water until smooth. Add the remainder of the ingredients and blend until smooth. May add chopped chives, if desired.

Onion-Cucumber Dressing
Mary Glick

1   cup sunflower seeds, soaked overnight and drained
1   medium cucumber, chopped
1   tablespoon onion powder
1   small red onion, chopped
$1/4$ cup raw unfiltered honey
$1/4$ cup fresh lemon juice
$1/4$ cup distilled water (adjust according to desired thickness)
    Celtic Sea Salt to taste (optional)

Place all ingredients in blender and blend until smooth.

Our Carrot Salad Dressing

$1/_2$ cup distilled water
$1/_2$ cup almonds, soaked overnight and drained
2   teaspoons raw unfiltered honey
$1/_2$ cup fresh pineapple
1   lemon including half of the yellow rind, juiced in a Champion™ or Green Star™

Blend almonds and water until smooth, then add remaining ingredients and blend to desired consistency.

Judy's Favorite Dressing
Judy Hartman

8   ounces freshly extracted carrot juice
1   tablespoon sunflower seeds, soaked overnight and drained
1   teaspoon sesame seeds, soaked overnight and drained
1   lemon, juiced
     Celtic Sea Salt to taste (optional)

Place all ingredients in blender and blend to desired consistency. If too thick, add more carrot juice or distilled water.

Soaked almonds or walnuts may be substituted for the seeds. Avocado or Udo's Choice Perfected Oil Blend™ may be added if desired.

Sunflower Seed-Onion Dressing

1	cup sunflower seeds, soaked overnight and drained
1	cucumber, seeded and chopped
1	tablespoon dehydrated onion flakes
1	small red onion
$^1/_4$	cup raw unfiltered honey
$^1/_4$	cup fresh lemon juice
	Celtic Sea Salt to taste (optional)

Place all ingredients in blender and process until smooth. If too thick, add a small amount of distilled water until desired consistency is reached.

Tomato Almond Dressing

1	cup almonds, soaked overnight and drained
2	medium ripe tomatoes
$^1/_4$	cup chopped red onion
2	lemons, juiced
	Celtic Sea Salt to taste (optional)

Place almonds in blender with enough distilled water to cover them. Process until smooth. Add remaining ingredients in the order given and process again. If too thin, add more almonds.

Creamy Carrot Dressing

1	cup distilled water
1	cup almonds, soaked overnight and drained
$^1/_4$	cup unhulled sesame seeds, soaked overnight and drained
1	tablespoon caraway seeds, soaked overnight and drained
$^1/_2$	cup fresh lemon juice
1	tablespoon dried oregano
1	teaspoon garlic powder
$^1/_2$	cup fresh chives or $^1/_4$ cup dried
1	garlic clove, peeled
1	bell pepper (red, orange or yellow)
1	medium carrot
1	tablespoon raw unfiltered honey
	Celtic Sea Salt to taste (optional)

Place distilled water, almonds and sesame seeds in blender and blend until smooth. Add remaining ingredients and blend again until smooth. This dressing thickens as it sits.

Green Onion Dressing

$1/_2$ cup distilled water
$1/_2$ cup fresh lemon juice
$3/_4$ cup almonds, soaked overnight and drained
$1/_4$ cup unhulled sesame seeds (white), soaked overnight and drained
2   teaspoons celery seed
1   teaspoon ground cardamom
2   tablespoons dill weed
2   teaspoons raw unfiltered honey (optional)
2-3   garlic cloves, peeled
1-3   tablespoons fresh parsley leaves (optional)
4-6   green onions or chives
    Celtic Sea Salt to taste (optional)

Blend distilled water, lemon juice, soaked almonds, sesame seeds and Celtic Sea Salt. Add other remaining ingredients except green onions and blend. Chop green onions or chives by hand and fold into dressing.

Tahini Dressing
Julie A. Gerbrandt

1   tablespoon tahini
1   tablespoon fresh lemon juice
    Celtic Sea Salt to taste (optional)

Whisk together, then toss with your salad.

Chive Dressing
Eleanor Brandow

1	cup distilled water
$^1/_2$	cup fresh lemon juice
$^3/_4$	cup almonds, soaked overnight and drained
$^1/_4$	teaspoon garlic powder
1	tablespoon fresh parsley
1	bunch of fresh chives
	Celtic Sea Salt to taste (optional)

Blend liquid ingredients, add soaked almonds, and blend until smooth, scrape sides. Add remaining ingredients and blend to desired consistency.

Basil Dressing

$1^1/_2$	cups distilled water
1	cup almonds, soaked overnight and drained
1	teaspoon onion powder
2	teaspoons dried basil (or $^1/_2$ to 1 cup fresh)
	Celtic Sea Salt to taste (optional)

Place all ingredients in blender and blend well.

Sunflower Seed Dressing

1   cup raw sunflower seeds, soaked overnight and drained
$1^{1}/_{4}$ cups distilled water
$1^{1}/_{2}$ teaspoons onion powder
$^{1}/_{4}$ teaspoon garlic powder
1   lemon, juiced
            Celtic Sea Salt to taste (optional)

Blend all ingredients for about two minutes, until smooth. Additional distilled water may be added to thin, if necessary.

Creamy Sunflower Seed Dressing

$2^{1}/_{2}$ cups distilled water
2   cups sunflower seeds, soaked overnight and drained
$^{1}/_{2}$ cup fresh lemon juice
2   teaspoons raw unfiltered honey
1-2   teaspoons garlic powder
1   teaspoon dried sweet basil
            Celtic Sea Salt to taste (optional)

Blend distilled water, sunflower seeds and lemon juice. Add remaining ingredients and blend well.

Bell Pepper Dressing

1	sweet bell pepper (red, yellow, orange, etc.)
1	cup almonds, soaked overnight and drained
$1/_2$	cup fresh lemon juice
2	teaspoons dried sweet basil
1	teaspoon raw unfiltered honey

Blend all ingredients until smooth. After the dressing sets, it thickens and can be used as a spread on sandwiches or raw crackers.

Garden Delight Dressing

Place the following ingredients in a blender and process until smooth:

$1/_3$	cup almonds, soaked overnight and drained
$1/_3$	cup distilled water
2	teaspoons extra virgin olive oil or flaxseed oil
$1/_2$	teaspoon lemon juice
	Celtic Sea Salt to taste (optional)

Chop the following and fold into the above mixture:

$1/_2$	cucumber, peeled, seeded and chopped
4-6	green onions, chopped
$1^1/_2$	tablespoons fresh parsley sprigs
2-4	radishes

Note: May be used as dip or dressing.

Sesame Seed (Tahini) Dressing

1	cup sesame seeds, soaked overnight and drained
$1/_4$	cup distilled water
2	garlic cloves, peeled and minced
1	lemon, peeled and diced
2	tablespoons cold-pressed extra virgin olive oil, or other light oil
$1/_3$	teaspoon cayenne (optional)

Grind seeds in blender or seed grinder until fine. Place ground seeds and remaining ingredients in a blender and process until smooth.

Almond Dressing

$2/_3$	cup distilled water
$1/_3$	cup fresh lemon juice
$3/_4$	cup almonds, soaked overnight and drained

Place in a blender and process until smooth, then add:

1	garlic clove, peeled (or 1 teaspoon garlic powder)
$1/_2$	teaspoon dried dill weed
2	teaspoons dried parsley flakes
	Celtic Sea Salt to taste (optional)

Stir to mix well, cover and chill.

Almost Thousand Island Dressing

1	cup almonds, soaked overnight and drained
1	cup distilled water
2-3	tablespoons fresh lemon juice
1	teaspoon onion powder
$\frac{1}{2}$	fresh ripe tomato
$\frac{1}{4}$	red or other sweet onion, minced

Blend all ingredients together except onion until smooth. Fold in minced onion.

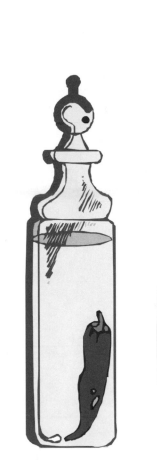
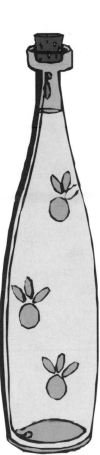

VEGETABLE BASED DRESSINGS

"He causeth the grass to grow for the cattle, and herb for the service of man:
that he may bring forth food out of the earth;..."

Psalm 104:14

Gazpacho Dressing

3	ripe tomatoes, quartered
1	tablespoon red onion, minced
2	celery stalks, cut in 2" pieces
1	red bell pepper, seeded and chopped
1	medium cucumber, peeled and seeded
1	tablespoon dried dill weed
2	tablespoons Udo's Choice Perfected Oil Blend™ or other mild oil
1	lemon, juiced

Combine all ingredients and process until smooth. Chill and serve.

French Dressing

$^1/_2$	cup ripe tomatoes, peeled and quartered
$^1/_4$	cup organic tomato paste, salt-free
2-3	tablespoons almond butter
1	teaspoon raw unfiltered honey
1	teaspoon onion powder
$^1/_4$	teaspoon garlic powder
2	tablespoons fresh lemon juice
$^1/_4$	cup distilled water
	Celtic Sea Salt to taste (optional)

Place all ingredients in blender and blend until creamy.

Tomato and Herb Delight Dressing

1   cup ripe tomatoes, peeled and quartered
$1/4$ teaspoon dill weed, scant
2   tablespoons fresh lemon juice
1   teaspoon fresh parsley (or $1/2$ teaspoon parsley flakes)
1   teaspoon onion powder
$1/3$ teaspoon garlic powder
$1/2$ teaspoon dried sweet basil
$1/4$ cup fresh red onion
            Celtic Sea Salt to taste (optional)

Blend all ingredients until smooth. Note: This dressing does not store well; best used fresh.

Garden Medley Dressing

$1/2$ cup freshly extracted juice*
$1/4$ cup almond meal
$1/2$ lemon, juiced
            Celtic Sea Salt to taste (optional)

*About 3 medium carrots, 1 or 2 green onions, and half of a ripe sweet bell pepper (red, yellow, orange, etc.)

Place all ingredients in a blender and process until smooth. Add more juice or almonds as needed for desired consistency.

Nature's Dressing
Ann Chitale

1	small bunch fresh basil, washed
1	small bunch fresh mint leaves, washed
1	small bunch fresh cilantro leaves, washed
1	small bunch fresh parsley leaves, washed
1	small bunch white seedless grapes
$^{1}/_{2}$	cup fresh lime juice
1	small ripe tomato, diced
2	garlic cloves, peeled

Place all ingredients in the food processor or blender and process until a dressing consistency is reached.

Author's note: For more dressings in the vegetable category, see *Recipes for Life ... from God's Garden.*

APPLE CIDER VINEGAR BASED DRESSINGS

"A word fitly spoken is like apples of gold in pictures of silver."
Proverbs 25:11

Author's note: In most recipes, fresh lemon juice can be substituted for raw unfiltered apple cider vinegar, if desired.

Versatile Marinade
Rita Carrigan
Christchurch, New Zealand

1	cup distilled water
$^1/_2$	cup raw unfiltered apple cider vinegar
1	large tablespoon raw unfiltered honey
1	teaspoon whole mustard seeds
1	teaspoon celery seeds

Place distilled water, apple cider vinegar and honey into a saucepan. Heat on lowest temperature; do not boil. When honey is dissolved, add mustard seeds and celery seeds and mix well. Remove from heat and allow mixture to cool.

Note: This is lovely added to coleslaw. Make the salad with a variety of vegetables, either chunky, or processed down for the elderly and those beginning to enjoy salads. This is enough to make a very large salad that keeps very well.

Sweet and Sour Dressing
Jerolyn Glanzer

$1/_4$	cup raw unfiltered honey
$3/_4$	cup raw unfiltered apple cider vinegar
$1^1/_2$	teaspoons celery seed
$1/_2$	cup cold pressed mayonnaise, Vegenaise™ or Nayonaise™
$1/_4$	cup mustard (optional)
$1^1/_2$	cups cold-processed extra virgin olive oil
4	tablespoons red or green onion, chopped
	Celtic Sea Salt to taste (optional)

Blend all ingredients in blender. Keeps very well in refrigerator. Yields 4 cups.

Cindy's Sweet and Sour Dressing
Cindy King

1	cup apple cider vinegar
$1/_2$	cup cold-pressed extra virgin olive oil
1	cup raw unfiltered honey
$1/_4$	cup brown rice malt syrup
1	garlic clove, minced
$1/_2$	teaspoon basil
$1/_2$	teaspoon oregano
$1/_2$	teaspoon ginger, minced
Dash	cayenne (optional)

Combine all ingredients. To allow flavors to mingle, store at room temperature until desired flavor is reached. Shake before using.

Oil and Vinegar Dressing
Diane Brandow

1	cup cold-pressed extra virgin olive oil
$1/_3$	cup raw unfiltered apple cider vinegar
2	teaspoons oregano
$1/_2$	teaspoon dry mustard (optional)
2	garlic cloves, peeled and crushed
	Celtic Sea Salt to taste (optional)

Combine all ingredients in a jar, cover tightly and shake to blend.

Basic Vinaigrette Dressing

$1/_4$	cup raw unfiltered apple cider vinegar
$1/_2$	cup olive oil, Udo's Choice Perfected Oil Blend™, or other oil
2	tablespoons distilled water
2	garlic cloves, peeled and minced
	Celtic Sea Salt to taste (optional)

Note: May also want to add one or more of the following:

1	teaspoon dried basil
1	teaspoon dried oregano
1	teaspoon dried thyme
1	teaspoon dried dill
1	teaspoon dried sage
$1/_2$	teaspoon lemon, lime, orange or grapefruit zest (shavings of the rind)

Place ingredients in a cruet, shake well and allow to sit for at least 15 minutes. Shake again before serving. Stores well.

Vinaigrette Dressing
Patricia Lee

$1/3$ cup raw unfiltered apple cider vinegar
2   garlic cloves, peeled
2   shallots, peeled and chopped or $1/4$ cup red or green onion
1   cup chopped flat-leafed Italian parsley
1   cup chopped cilantro
1   tablespoon raw unfiltered honey
1   teaspoon Celtic Sea Salt™ or unrefined sea salt (optional)
$1/4$ teaspoon cayenne pepper (optional)
1   pinch ground cloves (optional)
$1/2$ cup cold-pressed extra virgin olive oil

Place all of the ingredients in the blender and blend until completely smooth. Pour over salad and toss. Garnish with avocado slices and serve immediately.

Easy Vinaigrette
Laurie Libbon

$1/4$ cup Garlic Wine vinegar (optional)
$1/4$ cup balsamic vinegar or raw unfiltered apple cider vinegar
1   teaspoon Dijon mustard (optional)
1-2   garlic cloves
$1/4$ cup cold-pressed extra virgin olive oil

Mince the garlic cloves in a food processor and combine with the other ingredients. Mix well. Enjoy a wonderful tasty treat for so little effort!

Kay's Herb Dressing
Kay Frost

$1/_4$ cup Italian parsley
1   tablespoon fresh rosemary
2   tablespoons fresh cilantro leaves
2   tablespoons fresh thyme
$1/_4$ cup fresh basil
$1/_4$ cup raw unfiltered apple cider vinegar
3   tablespoons raw unfiltered honey
2   garlic cloves, peeled
$1/_2$ cup cold-pressed extra virgin olive oil

Place all ingredients except oil in a blender or food processor and puree. With machine running, drizzle in olive oil.

FRUIT BASED DRESSINGS

"In the midst of the street of it, and on either side of the river, was there the tree of life, which bare twelve manner of fruits, and yielded her fruit every month: and the leaves of the tree were for the healing of the nations."

Revelation 22:2

Tangy Mango Dressing

1	ripe mango
1	tablespoon fresh ginger, minced
$1/_4$	cup fresh apple juice or distilled water

Peel mango, combine with ginger and apple juice in blender and blend until creamy. Add more apple juice or distilled water if thinner dressing is desired.

Orange Dressing

1	cup fresh orange juice
$1/_4$	cup sesame seeds, soaked overnight and drained
$1/_4$	cup cold-pressed extra virgin olive oil or other mild oil
$1/_2$	lemon, juiced
$1/_4$	cup raw unfiltered honey
$1/_4$	teaspoon celery seed
$1/_8$	teaspoon cumin
$1/_8$	teaspoon paprika
	Celtic Sea Salt to taste (optional)

Grind sesame seeds in blender. Add rest of the ingredients and blend briefly at low speed.

Citrus Dressing

4   ounces sunflower seeds, soaked overnight and drained
           Oranges, lemons, grapefruit or any acid fruit, peeled

Using food processor, grind seeds to a meal. Add any of the above fruits and process until creamy.

Tarragon Dressing

1   cup fresh apple juice
$^1/_4$ cup lemon juice
1   teaspoon dry mustard (optional)
2   tablespoons dry tarragon
1   teaspoon garlic, peeled and minced

Combine liquids and dry mustard in a blender; process until well mixed. Remove from blender and add tarragon and garlic. Mix slightly until just combined. Cover and refrigerate at least two hours, allowing flavors to blend.

Raspberry Vinaigrette

Raspberry syrup base:

1   12 ounce package of unsweetened frozen strawberries
$^{1}/_{2}$ cup raw unfiltered honey

Place raspberries in a pan over low heat, and warm until thawed. Stir in honey and increase heat, bringing the mixture to a rolling boil. Boil for five minutes, stirring constantly. Remove from heat and strain through cheesecloth. After straining, discard raspberries. When the syrup has cooled, pour it into bottle and refrigerate.

Raspberry Vinaigrette Dressing:

$^{3}/_{4}$ cup cold-pressed extra virgin olive oil
$^{1}/_{2}$ cup raw unfiltered apple cider vinegar
5   tablespoons raspberry syrup from recipe above (adjust to taste)
1-2   garlic cloves, peeled and crushed
              Celtic Sea Salt to taste (optional)

Place all ingredients in a bowl and whip with a whisk until well blended.

Orange-Lemon Dressing

1   tablespoon arrowroot powder
1   tablespoon distilled water or fresh orange juice
2   cups fresh orange juice
1-2   tablespoons fresh lemon juice
$^1/_4$ cup maple syrup, brown rice malt syrup or raw unfiltered honey

Dissolve arrowroot powder in 1 tablespoon distilled water or orange juice. Set aside to allow arrowroot to dissolve. Simmer remaining orange juice and other liquids over low heat for 5 minutes or until heated, but not boiling. Add arrowroot mixture and simmer until thick, stirring constantly (about 3 minutes).

Berry Dressing

1   tablespoon arrowroot powder
1   tablespoon distilled water or fresh apple juice
$^1/_2$ cup fresh apple juice or distilled water
1-2   tablespoons fresh lemon juice
$^1/_4$ cup maple syrup, brown rice malt syrup or raw unfiltered honey
2   cups fresh berries

Dissolve arrowroot powder in 1 tablespoon distilled water or apple juice. Set aside to allow arrowroot to dissolve. Simmer remaining apple juice and other liquids over low heat for 5 minutes or until heated, but not boiling. Add arrowroot mixture and simmer until thick, stirring constantly (about 3 minutes). Remove from heat, cool and then fold in fresh berries.

Pineapple Dressing
Julie Zumach

1	tablespoon arrowroot powder
1	tablespoon distilled water or fresh pineapple juice
$\frac{1}{4}$	cup fresh pineapple juice
1	tablespoon raw unfiltered honey
1	tablespoon distilled water
1	tablespoon celery seed
$\frac{1}{2}$	teaspoon dry mustard (optional)
1	tablespoon minced onion

Dissolve arrowroot powder in 1 tablespoon distilled water or pineapple juice. Set aside to allow arrowroot to dissolve. Simmer remaining pineapple juice and other liquids over low heat for 5 minutes or until heated, but not boiling. Add arrowroot mixture and simmer until thick, stirring constantly (about 3 minutes). Remove from heat and fold in remaining ingredients. May add a handful of chopped pecans, if desired.

Mixed Fruit Dressing

1	cup fresh pineapple chunks
2	fresh peaches, apricots or apples
1-2	bananas
$\frac{1}{4}$	cup unsweetened coconut
$\frac{1}{2}$	cup pecans or walnuts
3-4	dates

Place all ingredients in blender and process until creamy.

Chunky Apple Dressing

3	cups fresh apple juice
1	cup distilled water
1	cup small apple chunks
4	tablespoons arrowroot powder
$^1/_2$	teaspoon lemon juice
$1^1/_4$	teaspoon coriander
$^1/_4$	teaspoon cardamom

Place all ingredients except apple chunks into blender and process until smooth. Pour mixture into saucepan and add apple chunks cook over medium heat until slightly thickened, stirring constantly. Cool before serving.

MISCELLANEOUS DRESSINGS

"O taste and see that the Lord is good: blessed is the man that trusteth in Him." Psalm 34:8

Vegenaise™ Salad Dressing
Martha Tracy

$3/_4$	cup cold-pressed extra virgin olive oil
2	tablespoons raw unfiltered apple cider vinegar
2	tablespoons herb seasoning
2	garlic cloves, peeled
2	tablespoons Vegenaise™ or Nayonaise™
$1/_2$	teaspoon stevia powder, raw unfiltered honey or other sweetener

Shake and serve. May add more apple cider vinegar if needed.

Ranch Dressing
Chef Bill Paul

1	14 ounce jar Nayonaise™
$1/_4$	cup raw unfiltered apple cider vinegar
2	tablespoons granulated garlic
4	tablespoons dried parsley flakes

Place all ingredients in a bowl and mix well. Store in covered container.

Sour Cream Dressing
Shirley Nielson

I love this recipe: I got it out of the vegetarian cookbook called *Tastefully Vegan*.

12	ounces firm Mori-Nu Tofu™
3-4	tablespoons raw unfiltered honey
$1/_3$	cup sunflower oil
3	tablespoons fresh lemon juice
	Celtic Sea Salt to taste (optional)

Place all ingredients in a blender and process until smooth. Seasonings or herbs can be added to vary the flavor. This dressing thickens after being refrigerated and lasts at least a week. Use any place you would use a salad dressing or mayonnaise.

French Dressing
Chef Bill Paul

$2/_3$	cup Nayonaise™
$1/_3$	cup catsup (from health food store)
Pinch	sea salt
Pinch	cayenne pepper

Place all ingredients in a bowl and mix well. Store in covered container.

Healthy Croutons
Gail Giustozzi

Cut Ezekiel™ (or other whole grain bread) into small squares, put them in a bowl, add a small amount of cold-pressed extra virgin olive oil, organic spices (onion powder, Italian seasoning, garlic powder, Celtic Sea Salt) and stir until all ingredients are blended. Air-dry or dehydrate if crunchy croutons are desired.

THE MOST IMPORTANT DECISION OF LIFE

Finally, let me share with you the most important decision you will ever make. Just as pure foods restore life to our physical bodies, Jesus (and *only* Jesus) brings life to our souls. Therefore, even though you may regain your health, live 120 years or more, there is one question for which we are all accountable. It is simply this: *"What have you done with Jesus?"* My friend, if you have not asked Jesus to be Lord and Master of your life and trusted Him as your personal Savior, won't you do so today? Our Lord Jesus Christ was born, lived, shed his sinless blood as full payment for your sins, died and was buried and rose again for your justification. By simply placing your faith and trust in Him and His shed blood *alone*, you can be saved and become a new creature in Christ.

If you need more information regarding this most important decision you will ever make, *please* contact us at Hallelujah Acres.

"For God so loved the world, that He gave His only begotten Son, that whosoever believeth in Him should not perish, but have everlasting life." John 3:16

GLOSSARY OF INGREDIENTS

Note: All food should be organic, if available.

Agar agar: A natural gelatin and thickening agent made from red algae that is boiled, pressed into a gel and then dried into flakes. It contains no calories and is colorless. Agar agar is 75 percent carbohydrate and is high in a type of fiber that passes through the body undigested, adding bulk to the diet and acting as a natural laxative. Flakes dissolve in hot liquids and thicken as they cool to room temperature or below. To prepare, add 4 tablespoons of flakes to 4 cups fruit juice or stock; boil, reduce heat and simmer 5 minutes or until dissolved.

Almond Butter (raw): A nut butter made from ground almonds. Almond butter is a good alternative to peanut butter and much easier for the body to digest. Can be found in health food stores.

Apple Cider Vinegar: Made from peels and cores of apples, unpasteurized, unheated with no chemicals added.

Arrowroot Powder: A tasteless powder made from West Indian arrowroot plant. Used as a thickener in place of corn starch. Use $1/4$ cup of *cold liquid* to 1 teaspoon arrowroot powder. Blend with liquid before adding to hot dishes to prevent clumps. Does not have to be heated to thicken. Most thickeners leave sauces white or cloudy, but arrowroot becomes transparent. Arrowroot is easier to digest than flour.

Balsamic Vinegar: A sweetish, aromatic vinegar made from the must of white grapes and aged in wooden barrels. (Transitional; organic raw apple cider vinegar is recommended.)

Basil: An herb that is always preferable fresh, but if fresh is not available, dried can be used. Basil is available in a wide variety of flavors from lemon to purple opal. It has a pungent flavor that has been described as a cross between cloves and licorice. Always store dried herbs in a dark place as sunlight deteriorates their freshness.

Bell Peppers: Are chunky in shape and hollow inside. They are a sweet variety of pepper and come in many colors such as red, yellow, orange, brown, purple and other colors. Green bell peppers are not ripe and not recommended. When ripe, bell peppers provide a wonderful source of vitamin C.

Bragg Liquid Aminos™: The manufacturer claims this is a non-heated, non-fermented, non-pasteurized soy product, similar in taste and appearance to soy sauce. Recent laboratory testing has shown that there is some naturally occurring monosodium glutamate (MSG) in Bragg Liquid Aminos that develops during processing.

Brewer's Yeast: a yeast used or suitable for brewing, a source of B complex vitamins.

Brown Rice Malt Syrup: A sweetener made from organic brown rice and naturally occurring enzymes from organic malted whole barley and water. Can be used in place of honey or maple syrup.

Caraway Seeds: Store seeds in refrigerator or freezer to prolong life as these seeds lose their flavor quickly.

Cayenne Pepper: An intense seasoning made from grinding small hot cayenne peppers. Caution: Very hot and can burn if too much is used; a little goes a long way.

Celtic Sea Salt: Sea salt harvested in the northwest area of France by the 2000 year old Celtic tradition of hand raking. Not subjected to refining and contains nearly 80 natural occurring elements as found in the sea waters.

Cilantro: Also called Chinese Parsley (the root of the plant is ground and the spice is called coriander). Cilantro resembles parsley in appearance except that it is pale in color. Most often used in Mexican and Asian dishes.

Coriander: Is made from the carrot-like root of the cilantro herb. It has a nutty flavor and delightful aroma. Tastes like lemon peel and sage combined.

Cumin: Member of the parsley family. Cumin is a pungent, strong flavored spice (whole or ground) that aids in digestion. Used in Mexican and Indian cooking. Warm robust flavor; use sparingly.

Curry Powder: A mixture of up to twenty spices, usually including cardamom, coriander, cumin and turmeric. Loses pungency quickly; buy in small amounts.

Dates: The oblong fruit of the date palm. There are many varieties of dates, but three best varieties for food preparation are medjool, khadrawi and honey.

Date Sugar: A natural sweetener from dried ground dates. Can be used in recipes calling for a sweetener. Date sugar has a coarse, brown texture and is not as sweet as refined sugar. Heated during processing; therefore it is not considered raw.

Dulse: A burgundy colored sea vegetable. Wash and soak prior to adding to foods. Can also be washed, dried and ground into flakes or a corse powder. Like kelp, dulse can be found in shakers in some health food stores.

Fennel Seeds: These seeds have a licorice-like flavor, are a good seasoning and aid in digestion.

Flax Seeds: Contain high concentrations of beneficial oils. Flax seeds may be ground and used in beverages or sprinkled on salads. May also be used as a thickener.

Garlic: a hardy plant and member of the amaryllis family. The bulb of this plant consists of several small bulbs or cloves. Garlic has a pungent flavor that is distinctive. Fresh garlic is best, far better than powdered or pre-peeled in jars.

Ginger: A reed-like plant grown mostly in tropical countries. The plant's rhizome (root) is dried and ground into a powder or used fresh. Ginger has a pungent spicy flavor (a little goes a long way.) Fresh ginger root is best stored in the refrigerator or freezer, where it will keep several months.

Herbs: Always use fresh herbs when available. Try basil, oregano, dill, tarragon, chives, mint, thyme, cilantro, fennel, garlic, Italian parsley, marjoram, rosemary, sage, ginger root, or your favorite.

Honey (raw unfiltered): A sweet liquid produced by bees from the nectar collected from flowers. Very concentrated sweetener; should not be given to babies as their digestive systems are not developed enough to digest it. Some prefer not to use honey as it comes from an animal source. If using honey, buy raw unfiltered honey from a local beekeeper. Clover and wildflower honey have the mildest flavor.

Kelp: Seaweed also known as kombu. Can be bought in granules or sheets. Can be used as a salt replacement.

Kudzu or kuzu: A natural gelling and thickening agent. Made from a root that grows wild in Japan.

Lemons: Fresh lemon juice can be used to replace vinegar in most recipes. Buy fresh lemons only. Used to flavor and preserve food.

Maple granules or sprinkles: A granulated sweetener made from pure maple syrup. Because of processing, this is not a raw food.

Nama Shoyu™: Traditional unpasteurized soy sauce from Japan made from wheat. Similar in flavor to Bragg Liquid Aminos™.

Nayonaise™: Natural mayonnaise substitute found in health food stores. Free of egg, dairy and refined sugar.

Nutritional yeast: Usually golden or bright yellow in color, but can be a dull brown. Nutritional yeast is 5o percent protein and comes in powder or flakes. Adds a rather cheesy taste to dishes and in hot dishes should be added at the end of cooking. Can be sprinkled on salads, dressings or main course dishes. Good source of B vitamins.

Nutmeg: Hard, aromatic seed of East India. Used in a grated form as a spice with a warm, hearty and sweet aroma.

Oregano: An aromatic herb that is a member of the mint family. The leaves of the plant are used to lend an Italian flavor to dishes. Dried is more pungent that fresh.

Paprika: A red powdery condiment derived from dried, ripe sweet peppers. Often used to add flavor and color.

Parsley: An herb native to the Mediterranean. Parsley will have either curled leaf clusters (French) or flat compound leaves (Italian). The leaves of this culinary herb are often used as a garnish or to add flavor.

Pine Nuts (pignoli or pignolia): The edible soft white nut or seed from pine cones, used primarily for sauces or dressings. Very short shelf life; should be stored in the freezer.

Raisins: Organic Thompson or Monukka varieties are best. "Golden" raisins are those that have usually had the color removed with a bleaching agent.

Scallions: A scallion is any onion that does not form a large bulb, such as green onions, shallots or leeks. Scallions are slightly milder than red, yellow or white onions. Green onions are also sometimes called spring onions.

Sea Salt: Unrefined, solar evaporated (sun-dried) sea salt; high in natural trace minerals but not sodium chloride. Contains no added chemicals. If using sea salt, choose a reputable source so that you know the salt is pure and unadulterated. Use sparingly. Note: Avoid all table salt. Most table salt is stripped of all of its nutrients and natural minerals that are then chemically added back during processing.

Sesame Seed, hulled: Sesame seeds whose hulls have been removed.

Sesame Seed, unhulled: Sesame seeds whose hulls have not been removed.

Shallots: Related to the onion and have a similar taste. Shallots consist of a small cluster of bulbs.

Squash: Summer squash: crookneck, zucchini and pattypan have edible skins. Winter squash: acorn, butternut and hubbard have a non-edible hard, thick skin.

Stevia: An herb related to the daisy family that is native to Central America. Stevia extract is 300 times as sweet as table sugar without the harmful side effects of other sugar substitutes. Comes in powder or liquid form.

Tahini, raw: A seed butter made from lightly toasted hulled, sesame seeds. It is light in color and adds flavor to soups, potato salad, spreads or even sweet treats. Tahini is not the same as sesame butter that is thicker, darker and made from unhulled sesame seeds. Can be used instead of nut butters.

Tamari: A wheat-free, unpasteurized soy sauce. Tamari is naturally fermented with no alcohol added.

Tarragon vinegar: Raw unfiltered apple cider vinegar to which tarragon has been added and allowed to sit for several days, allowing the flavors to mingle.

Tofu: Bland cheese-like substance made from soybeans or soy flour; used as a meat replacement. Tofu is very high in protein and should be used sparingly.

Udo's Choice Perfected Oil Blend™: Udo's is a cold-pressed organic blend of flax seed, sunflower seed and sesame seed oils, as well as oils from wheat germ, oat germ and rye germ. Udo's Choice Perfected Oil Blend is not a cooking oil; do not heat.

Vegenaise™: A natural mayonnaise substitute found in the cold case of many health food stores. Vegenaise is free from egg and dairy and contains no refined sweeteners. Since some Vegenaise™ is made with other oils, always check the label to make sure that the product is made from grapeseed oil.

Wakame: A pale green seaweed also called alaria. Comes in sheets and gives soups, salads and other foods a delightful flavor.

INDEX OF RECIPES

AVOCADO BASED DRESSINGS

OIL BASED DRESSINGS

SEED AND NUT BASED DRESSINGS

VEGETABLE BASED DRESSINGS

APPLE CIDER VINEGAR BASED DRESSINGS

FRUIT BASED DRESSINGS

MISCELLANEOUS

Other Inspirational Books on Health from Hallelujah Acres

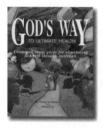

God's Way to Ultimate Health
This book has everything you need to know about how to return to God's original plan for nourishing the human body. Read what the Bible says about diet and how this biblical wisdom is supported by modern science and hundreds of real life testimonials. Also an entire section of recipes and tips by Rhonda Malkmus on how to set up your own natural foods kitchen. Many people say these 282 pages have saved their lives!

#202   1-3 copies $18.95   4-16 copies $15.16
           17-50 copies $13.27   51+ copies $11.37

Recipes for Life. . . From God's Garden
This book by Rhonda Malkmus is the perfect companion piece to God's Way to Ultimate Health, because it begins where the theory and rationale for the diet leaves off. Healthy food tastes wonderful, and this huge 8 ½ x 11 inch spiral bound book proves it with more than 400 nutritious and delicious recipes! It has important chapters on how to feed children and young adults, and even a section on feeding babies. Includes detailed index.

#203   1-3 copies $24.95   4-14 copies $19.96
           15-45 copies $17.47   46+ copies $14.97

Why Christians Get Sick
By Rev. George Malkmus, this book is very helpful in introducing Christians to a natural diet and lifestyle. Letters are received daily from all over the world from people helped by this book, which is now in its 21st printing. It is written on a solid biblical foundation with more than 150 Bible verses.

English #201, Spanish #201S, Korean #201K

1-3 copies $8.95   2-10 copies $7.16
11-49 copies $6.27   50+ copies $5.37

Children and the Hallelujah Diet Audio Cassette
Dr. Joel Robbins shares what he has learned about health and children. In this tape of his address to Health Ministers, you'll learn why you're letting your family down if you don't get your kids on a healthy diet. Dr. Robbins also provides helpful suggestions on how to get your children on a living diet, as well as how to keep them there.
Audio Cassette #232 - $9.95

Hallelujah Acres Food Show

Hallelujah Acres presents the Hallelujah Food Show designed to help people transition to a healthy diet and lifestyle. Your host, Dave Ridgeway, shares many of the recipe ideas found in the "Recipe for Life... from God's Garden" recipe book. All videos are professionally produced and range in time from 25 to 53 minutes.

8 Episodes VHS Video - $14.95 each

#221 Let's Get Started
#223 Choices, Variety, and Convenience
#224 Basics for Great Recepies
#226 Feeding Our Children
#225 The Hallelujah Diet at Work and on the Road
#227 A Day on the Hallelujah Diet
#228 Holidays and Special Occasions
#229 Eating Outdoors

How to Eliminate Sickness Video

This professionally-produced videotape was recorded on-site in Tulsa, Oklahoma, in April 1999 at the Tulsa Bible Prophecy Conference. This 2 ½-hour seminar contains the information that Rev. Malkmus has found through his research and study. It is the seminar that Hallelujah Acres' founder has taught throughout the United States and Canada, and it covers the basics of why we get sick and how to nourish our bodies in order to restore them to health. This video will change your thinking forever as to what is nutrition and what is not. You must see this remarkable video!

VHS Video #266 - $24.95

The Miraculous Self-Healing Body

Listen as five leading health experts discuss the dangers of the Standard American Diet as they present evidence that improper diet is the leading cause of almost every physical ailment. Dr. Neil Barnard, Dr. Joel Fuhrman, Dr. John McDougall, Dr. Russell Blaylock, and Rev. George Malkmus reveal the secrets to a healthy, vital, disease-free body. Very powerful video!
VHS Video #219 - $17.95

Get Healthy! is Hallelujah Acres' new total health training program. This nine lesson course covers every part of the Hallelujah Diet and Lifestyle. Call Hallelujah Acres to find a Health Minister teaching classes in your area.

ORDER FORM

Make copies of this order form so that you may reuse it. Mail orders to:
Hallelujah Acres, PO Box 2388, Shelby, NC 28151 or call 1-704-481-1700

Customer Name:_____

Address:_____

City:_____ State:_____ ZIP:_____

Telephone: (_____) _____ - _____ Email: _____

Credit Card Number: _____

Signature:_____ Exp. Date:_____

Qty.	Item	Item Name	Price Each	Total

O **Check**	Sub-total
O **Money Order**	6% Sales Tax (NC residents only)
O **VISA**	
O **Mastercard**	Shipping (Express Shipping Extra)
O **Discover**	
O **American Express**	Total